S0-AYO-480

NEW MEXICO

The Land of Enchantment

Ruth Bjorklund, Ellen H. Todras, and Gerry Boehme

Cavendish
Square
New York

OCT 2 6 2016

Published in 2016 by Cavendish Square Publishing, LLC
243 5th Avenue, Suite 136, New York, NY 10016

Copyright © 2016 by Cavendish Square Publishing, LLC

Third Edition   **3 9082 13139 5926**

Website: cavendishsq.com

This publication represents the opinions and views of the author based on his or her personal experience, knowledge, and research. The information in this book serves as a general guide only. The author and publisher have used their best efforts in preparing this book and disclaim liability rising directly or indirectly from the use and application of this book.

CPSIA Compliance Information: Batch #WS15CSQ

All websites were available and accurate when this book was sent to press.

Library of Congress Cataloging-in-Publication Data

Boehme, Gerry.
New Mexico / Gerry Boehme, Ruth Bjorklund, and Ellen Todras.
pages cm. — (It's my state!)
Includes bibliographical references and index.
ISBN 978-1-62713-210-7 (hardcover) ISBN 978-1-62713-212-1 (ebook)
1. New Mexico—Juvenile literature. I. Bjorklund, Ruth. II. Todras, Ellen H., 1947- III. Title.

F796.3.B64 2016
978.9—dc23

2014049274

Editorial Director: David McNamara
Editor: Fletcher Doyle
Copy Editor: Rebecca Rohan
Art Director: Jeffrey Talbot
Designer: Stephanie Flecha
Senior Production Manager: Jennifer Ryder-Talbot
Production Editor: Renni Johnson
Photo Research by J8 Media

Printed in the United States of America

NEW MEXICO

CONTENTS

State Bird: Greater Roadrunner

Also known as the chaparral bird, the greater roadrunner is a desert bird that eats insects, lizards, and snakes. It would rather run or walk than fly. The roadrunner can race at speeds up to 15 miles per hour (24 kilometers per hour) and is quick enough to chase and devour a rattlesnake.

State Flower: Yucca

The yucca is a spiky plant that can grow as tall as 30 feet (9 meters). It has white flowers on the end of its long slender stalk. Early settlers used the roots to make soap. The leaves were used to make rope and twine.

State Fossil: Coelophysis

Coelophysis (see-loh-FIE-sis) lived about 228 million years ago. This meat-eating dinosaur was about 9 feet (2.7 m) long, with a pointed head, jagged teeth, and three claws on each hand. Its name means "hollow form," because its bones were hollow. Scientists discovered hundreds of *Coelophysis* skeletons near Ghost Ranch, New Mexico, in the 1940s.

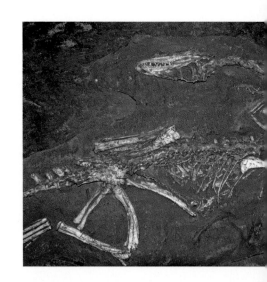

NEW MEXICO
POPULATION: 2,059,179

★ State Gem: **Turquoise**

This beautiful and valuable gemstone gets its color from copper, iron, and a green mineral called variscite inside it. The Navajo and **Pueblo** Native Americans have been mining turquoise for ornamental use for hundreds of years. Making jewelry using turquoise set in silver is a big industry in New Mexico today.

★ State Tree: **Piñon Pine**

Piñon (PEEN-yon) pines grow slowly, but they can reach heights of up to 35 feet (11 m). The depth of the root system below ground can be equal to the tree's height. The piñon is prized for the sweet smell of its wood and for its tasty seed, the pine nut.

★ State Vegetables: **Frijoles and Chiles**

The Pueblo Native Americans began growing frijoles (free-HO-lays), or pinto beans, centuries ago. In the 1500s, Spanish settlers brought chiles (spicy red or green peppers) to New Mexico from Mexico. The two vegetables have been key ingredients in the diet of the area's residents ever since.

White Sands National Monument includes
275 square miles (712 square kilometers) of dunes.

The Land of Enchantment

1

N ew Mexico is a land of natural wonders. From soaring mountains to deep, dark caves, from vast golden deserts to red canyon walls, the land glows under dazzling skies. Author Charles Lummis has written, "Most of New Mexico, most of the year, is a … harmony of browns and grays, over which the enchanted light of its blue skies casts an eternal spell …" Visitors and residents alike can see why New Mexico is called the "Land of Enchantment."

New Mexico is located in the Mountain Time Zone of the United States. It shares its borders with five other states as well as one foreign country (Mexico). Four states— New Mexico, Colorado, Utah and Arizona—meet in an area known as the "Four Corners." Each state is one corner. This is the only place in the United States where four states come together. If you are very agile, you can have your photo taken at Four Corners Monument with your legs in two states and your arms in the other two. It's not a very dignified position, but lots of fun to try.

New Mexico is divided into thirty-three counties. Although New Mexicans love the natural beauty of the state's landscapes, today about two-thirds of them live in urban areas. Albuquerque is the state's largest city, with more than 545,000 residents. Santa Fe, the state capital, has a population of about sixty-nine thousand.

NEW MEXICO
COUNTY MAP

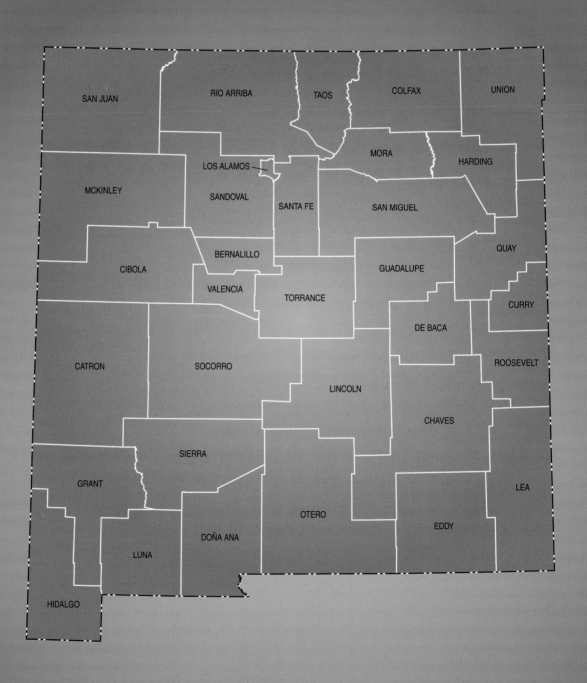

SAN JUAN

RIO ARRIBA

TAOS

COLFAX

UNION

MORA

HARDING

LOS ALAMOS

MCKINLEY

SANDOVAL

SANTA FE

SAN MIGUEL

QUAY

BERNALILLO

GUADALUPE

CIBOLA

VALENCIA

CURRY

TORRANCE

DE BACA

ROOSEVELT

CATRON

SOCORRO

LINCOLN

CHAVES

SIERRA

GRANT

LEA

OTERO

EDDY

DOÑA ANA

LUNA

HIDALGO

NEW MEXICO
POPULATION BY COUNTY

County	Population	County	Population	County	Population
Bernalillo	662,564	Harding	695	Roosevelt	19,846
Catron	3,725	Hidalgo	4,894	Sandoval	131,561
Chaves	65,645	Lea	64,727	San Juan	130,044
Cibola	27,213	Lincoln	20,497	San Miguel	29,393
Colfax	13,750	Los Alamos	17,950	Santa Fe	144,170
Curry	48,376	Luna	25,095	Sierra	11,988
De Baca	2,022	McKinley	71,492	Socorro	17,866
Doña Ana	209,233	Mora	4,881	Taos	32,937
Eddy	53,829	Otero	63,797	Torrance	16,383
Grant	29,514	Quay	9,041	Union	4,549
Guadalupe	4,687	Rio Arriba	40,246	Valencia	76,569

Source: US Bureau of the Census, 2010

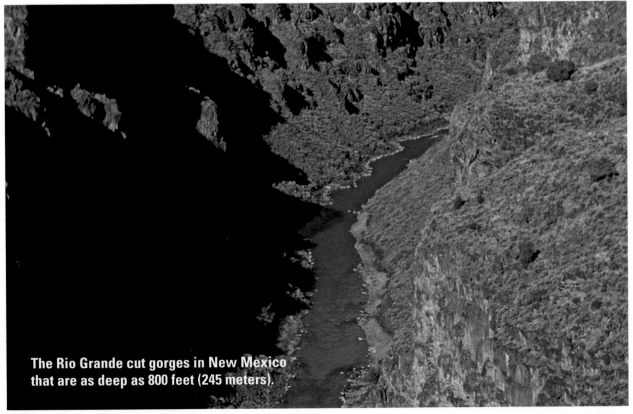

The Rio Grande cut gorges in New Mexico that are as deep as 800 feet (245 meters).

Enchanted Mesa rises more than 400 feet (120 meters) above west–central New Mexico.

New Mexico Borders	
North:	Colorado
South:	Texas
	Mexico
East:	Oklahoma
	Texas
West:	Arizona
Northwest:	Utah

The Landscape

New Mexico ranks thirty-sixth among all states in terms of population, but it is the nation's fifth-largest state in terms of size. Its land area is 121,298 square miles (314,160 square kilometers), barely enough to hold all of the state's diverse features. Most of New Mexico is filled with mountain ranges, deserts, and huge forests. So it's not surprising that, with its large size and relatively small population, New Mexico falls near the back of the pack (forty-fifth among all states) in population density, with only 17.2 people on average living in each square mile (6.62 per sq km).

Many of the state's residents are crowded into Bernalillo County. Despite being the second smallest county in the state, Bernalillo is home to about one-third of the total state population. That's mainly because Albuquerque, the largest city in New Mexico, is within the county's borders.

New Mexico's landscape is extraordinary. The majestic Rocky Mountains tower over the northern part of the state, while the vast prairies of the Great Plains cover eastern New Mexico. The Rio Grande (Spanish for "big river") flows north to south through the center of the state. In other parts of New Mexico, there are mountain ranges, **mesas** (broad, flat-topped hills with cliff-like sides), canyons, valleys, caverns, rivers, and **arroyos** (dry riverbeds that fill with water when it rains or when snow melts).

Record of Volcanoes

New Mexico surprisingly offers a detailed and diverse record of volcanic activity, perhaps more than any other state. Many familiar and distinctive New Mexico landscapes are composed of volcanoes and volcanic rocks.

The black, barren, lunar landscapes around Grants and Carrizozo are recent lava flows, and the black, flat-topped mesas around Albuquerque are remnants of older lava flows. Mount Taylor and Capulin Mountain are volcanoes. Los Alamos is built on the flank of a volcano so large that it is best seen from space. Ship Rock and Cabezon Peak are eroded remnants of volcanoes.

Although not as easy to recognize, many of the rocks in the Gila Mountains and other southern and western New Mexico mountain ranges are volcanic. While some volcanic rocks in New Mexico are very young in scientific terms, perhaps only 3,800 years old, others found in northern New Mexico are more than a billion years old.

New Mexico's climate helps preserve its geologic features. While most other volcanic areas in North America have been damaged by water and severe weather, New Mexico's dry and temperate climate acts like a giant air conditioner, forming a natural museum to protect its volcanic phenomena. These phenomena are interesting facts or

Green Volcano rises to the west of Albuquerque.

events that can be studied. Even those volcanoes that are eroded are really only deeply cut, not weathered, and the surface features are still intact for examination. In New Mexico, you can walk through the interior of many volcanoes and still examine their relatively uneroded surface features.

World Heritage Sites are special cultural or natural sites chosen by the United Nations Educational, Scientific, and Cultural Organization (**UNESCO**). These sites are considered among the most important in the entire world. The Great Wall of China and the pyramids of Egypt are some examples. New Mexico has three World Heritage Sites: Carlsbad Caverns, Chaco Canyon, and the Taos Pueblo.

Rocky Mountains and Great Plains

The southern end of the Rocky Mountains covers northern New Mexico. The Rio Grande flows through the southern Rockies and splits it into ranges that have been given their own names. One of these ranges is the Sangre de Cristo Mountains. This is where snow-covered Wheeler Peak rises. At 13,161 feet (4,011 m), it is the tallest point in the state. The landscape in New Mexico's mountains includes canyons, ancient lava flows, and high mountain meadows. Nearby, there are cities and towns such as Los Alamos, Taos, and Santa Fe.

Grasslands cover New Mexico's Great Plains region. Short, hardy bunchgrasses such as blue grama and buffalo grass grow as far as the eye can see. The southeastern section is called El Llano Estacado, which means "staked plains" in Spanish. Some say the term comes from Spanish explorers who long ago pounded stakes into the ground to mark their routes. With an average of seventeen people per square mile, it is a remote land of open spaces and vast ranches.

Lemonade Bush

A drink that tastes a lot like lemonade can be made from the berries of the three-leaf sumac. From this, the bush gets its common name, the Lemonade Bush.

More than one hundred years ago, ranchers began raising cattle in this area. The cattle stripped the prairie of its grasses. In times of drought, the grass would not grow, cattle could not eat, and ranches failed. In some parts of the region, farmers plowed the land to grow crops, but many farms also failed in times of drought. In what is now New Mexico's Kiowa National Grassland, the US government bought ranches and farms and tried to replant the prairie.

The grass did not grow well at first, so government officials turned to a biologist named Allan Savory. Savory said that, historically, healthy prairies needed bison (also called

The federal government has worked to restore the prairie of the Kiowa National Grassland in northeastern New Mexico.

buffalo) in order to thrive. He noted that when wild bison fed on prairie grass, they stayed in herds, ate the grass to the ground, and stomped on what they did not eat. The trampled grass turned into sod, a rich soil in which new grass could grow. Cattle do not usually graze in the same way as wild buffalo. So Savory suggested that cattle should be fenced together to graze on the land, so that they too could trample the prairie grass. It worked. Native grasses and wildflowers that had not bloomed in decades now flourish in the Kiowa National Grassland.

The Intermountain Region

The intermountain region covers southern, central, and western New Mexico. The area has several ranges, including the Zuni, Mogollon, Cibola, Sandia, Guadalupe, and San Andres Mountains. Many of these ranges are named after Native American tribes. The Rio Grande brings life-giving water from the Rocky Mountains all the way to the Mexican border. Other rivers, such as the San Juan, the Gila (HEE-la), and the Pecos, nourish a variety of plant and animal life. In other parts of the region, there are high mesas, caves, canyons, and badlands (areas with large rock formations and very little plant life).

Bandelier National Monument

Carlsbad Caverns

Cumbres & Toltec Scenic Railroad

1. Bandelier National Monument

Bandelier National Monument includes rugged volcanic landscapes and evidence of human presence going back over eleven thousand years. Dwellings carved into the soft rock cliffs pay tribute to the early days of a culture that still survives in the surrounding communities.

2. Billy The Kid Museum

Famous outlaw Billy the Kid was shot and killed when he was twenty-one at the nearby Fort Sumner State Monument by Sheriff Pat Garrett. The museum hosts the Kid's rifle, horse-riding equipment, and the original Wanted poster.

3. Carlsbad Caverns

A World Heritage site, Carlsbad Caverns National Park is hidden mostly underground and comprises nearly 120 known caves. Over time, sulfuric acid dissolved into the surrounding limestone, creating stunning rock formations.

4. Chaco Canyon

Located near the Four Corners region, World Heritage site Chaco Canyon National Historic Park explores the lifestyle of the prehistoric Chacoan people who inhabited the area from 850 to 1250 CE. The park features massive, well-preserved pueblo buildings, some with two stories.

5. Cumbres & Toltec Scenic Railroad

This narrow gauge heritage railroad runs between Chama, New Mexico and Antonito, Colorado. It is the highest steam railroad in the nation. Constructed in 1880–1881, this train climbs the 10,015-foot (3,052 m) Cumbres Pass.

6. Georgia O'Keeffe Museum

The Georgia O'Keeffe Museum in Santa Fe celebrates the work of the famed New Mexico artist. The museum houses more than 1,100 paintings, sculptures, photographs, sketches, and drawings, and is the only US museum dedicated to an internationally known female artist.

Georgia O'Keeffe Museum

7. International UFO Museum

The International **UFO** Museum is located in the famous town of Roswell, the site where some believe an unidentified flying object (UFO) crashed in 1947. The museum features information about the supposed crash and other reported alien encounters around the world.

8. Sandia Peak Tramway

One of the most popular attractions in Albuquerque, the Sandia Peak Tramway carries passengers nearly 3 miles (4.8 km) to the peak of Sandia Mountain at 10,378 feet (3,163 m) and provides great views of the Rio Grande Valley.

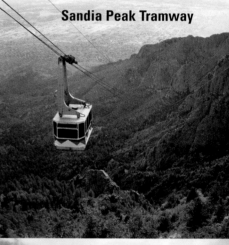

Sandia Peak Tramway

9. Taos Pueblo

Just north of the city of Taos, Taos Pueblo is the only living Native American community that is both a UNESCO World Heritage Site and a National Historic Landmark. The multi-storied **adobe** buildings have been continuously inhabited for more than one thousand years.

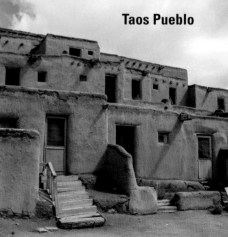

Taos Pueblo

10. White Sands National Monument

White Sands National Monument is one of the most stunning landscapes in the state. Gleaming white gypsum sand has built up into dunes up to 60 ft (18.2 m) high.

Thousands of years of wind, dust, and rain have carved the formations of the Bisti Badlands.

Near the Pecos River in southern New Mexico is Carlsbad Caverns, one of the most famous cave systems in the world. Its Big Room is the largest underground chamber in North America. Visitors who stay until sunset can watch hundreds of thousands of Mexican free-tailed bats stream out of the caves. Scientists say the bats can eat eleven tons (ten metric tons) of insects on a summer night.

Another natural wonder in New Mexico is the 275 square miles (712 sq km) of dunes in the southern part of the state, now protected as part of the White Sands National Monument. Billions of tons of a white mineral called selenite, or gypsum, form these dunes, which pile up when the winds blow.

Western New Mexico has many wilderness areas. The country's first national wilderness is among them. The Gila Wilderness, part of the Gila National Forest, is where ancient people once lived in cliff dwellings. It is also a land of dry mesas, steep canyons, and badlands. From the rock formations called the Bisti Badlands in the northwestern corner of the state, you can travel roads seven hundred years old into Chaco Canyon. There, ancient people built a huge city in the canyon walls. Visitors to the Chaco Culture National Historical Park can still see the remains of this amazing accomplishment.

The Climate

The climate of New Mexico is generally mild, sunny, and dry. The average rainfall is about 13 inches (33 centimeters) per year. Winters are drier than summers. Temperatures and precipitation (the amount of water an area receives in the form of rain, snow, sleet, and hail) can vary widely from day to night, from summer to winter, from mountain to valley, and from north to south. The south gets about 8 inches (20 cm) of rainfall each year. But in the north, the total is closer to 30 inches (76 cm).

Storm clouds bring lightning and often heavy rain in summer.

In winter, cold air moves south from Canada and brings snow to the mountains, as well as occasional snow to the valleys. Year-round average temperatures are 50 to 60 degrees Fahrenheit (10 to 16 degrees Celsius). But temperatures can rise to 100°F (38°C) in the summer and fall below 0°F (−18°C) in the winter.

Photographer Ansel Adams once remarked, "New Mexico's summer thunderstorms are the power of the land." During the summer months, brief, heavy thunderstorms are common. New Mexico has more lightning strikes than any other state. As one resident has said, "The lightning is absolutely terrifying; it's so right there in front of you. We just stay inside until it's over." When thunderclouds pour rain, the arroyos fill quickly and often create dangerous flash floods. But in dry regions, the thunderclouds bring more wind than rain, stirring the dust into tornado-like swirls called dust devils.

For the past several years, many states in the Southwest have suffered from extremely dry conditions, leading to water shortages and changes in the landscape. New Mexico has been one of the states hit the hardest. The years 2012–2014 have been the driest and warmest since record-keeping began in 1895. The state will require several years of normal rainfall to erase the effects.

Dry Land

New Mexico has the lowest percentage of surface water of any state. Only 0.2 percent of its total surface area is covered by water.

Wildlife

Many different types of plants and animals can be found throughout New Mexico. The forests in the mountain regions are lush with pine, fir, aspen, and spruce trees. Clear streams and lakes are filled with Rio Grande trout. Roaming freely in the high country are elk, mule deer, bobcats, and mountain lions. Coyotes, bighorn sheep, and bears inhabit the land as well. The American black bear is the official state mammal. Black bears roam the state's woodlands, eating berries, nuts, fruits, and other plants, as well as rodents and other small animals. They have coats that can be either brown or black, and they can weigh from 200 to 600 pounds (from 90 to 270 kilograms).

In Their Own Words

"Arriving in New Mexico ... Well! Well! Well! ... This is wonderful. No one told me it was like this!"
—Artist Georgia O'Keeffe

New Mexico's deserts and canyons are filled with cactuses and other plants that thrive in the hot and dry conditions. Lizards, snakes, spiders, scorpions, and small rodents scamper across the dusty ground. In the sky, eagles and hawks soar in search of prey. The climate presents a challenge to some nesting desert birds. They do not always sit on their eggs to keep them warm. Sometimes they will spread their wings above their nests to block the sun and keep the eggs cool.

Along the Rio Grande, in the Bosque del Apache National Wildlife Refuge, hundreds of thousands of birds gather. Many types of birds that spend the summer farther north

Sandhill cranes fly great distances to spend their winters in New Mexico.

There were an estimated fifty-three Mexican gray wolves in the wild in New Mexico in 2014, up from zero in 1998.

fly south to Bosque del Apache for the winter. Visitors to the refuge can see tropical songbirds, raptors (birds of prey), ducks, geese, and giant sandhill cranes. Lucky bird-watchers may even catch a glimpse of endangered species, such as the American whooping crane.

Endangered Wildlife

New Mexico's plants and animals are an important part of the state. Many residents try to help the state's wildlife in a number of ways. They conserve scarce resources such as water, protect the natural habitats of plants and animals, and make sure that threatened or endangered animals are not hunted. A species is considered threatened when its numbers are reduced and it is at risk of dying out altogether. There are many species of threatened or endangered animals in New Mexico. These include the Chiricahua leopard frog, the New Mexican ridge-nosed rattlesnake, Baird's sparrow, and the white-sided jackrabbit.

The US Fish and Wildlife Service has been working to restore the populations of some endangered species in New Mexico. For example, the Mexican gray wolf was nearly extinct by the 1970s. The Fish and Wildlife Service began to breed the wolves in captivity. In 1998, the service began releasing these wolves into the wild. Although the Mexican gray wolf remains endangered, its population is increasing.

10 KEY PLANTS AND ANIMALS

Black Bear

Century Plant

Cutthroat Trout

1. American Pika

Also known as the cony or rock rabbit, the American pika is part of the hare and rabbit family. It looks like a guinea pig, lives in high, rocky places, and is known for its squeaking sounds.

2. Black Bear

New Mexico's state animal, black bears live in most forested areas in the state. They can weigh more than two hundred pounds and are **omnivorous**, eating both plants and animals. Black bears can also be colored cinnamon, brown, or even blond.

3. Blue Grama Grass

Blue grama grass grows well in dry, warm conditions, and stands up very well to animal grazing. The official state grass, blue grama is important because its dense, shallow root mass holds down the soil and keeps it from blowing away.

4. Century Plant

The century plant first grows tough, stiff leaves that store food and water. Then, using the stored nutrients, a flower stalk appears. Native Americans roasted and ate the stalks and used them to make flutes, rope, rugs, baskets, and cloth.

5. Cutthroat Trout

Cutthroat (Rio Grande) trout is found in cold mountain streams and lakes of northern New Mexico. It is named for the red streak under its throat. Anglers like its fighting spirit. The Cutthroat population has declined but the state has been working to protect it.

NEW MEXICO ★ ★ ★

Javelina

Prickly Pear Cactus

Western Banded Gecko

6. Javelina

The javelina, or collared peccary, is the only native wild boar in the United States. Javelinas have large heads with pig-like snouts, slender legs, and sharp, straight tusks. Their name comes from the Spanish *javelina*, which means "javelin" or "spear."

7. Prickly Pear Cactus

Sharp yellow or red spines cover the prickly pear cactus's flat, fleshy pads, which look like leaves but are actually branches. Desert animals seek its pads for the water inside while people prepare them as a vegetable called *nopalitos*.

8. Tarantula Hawk

Tarantula hawks are spider wasps whose powerful sting is one of the most painful in the world. Tarantula hawks capture tarantulas as food for their larvae.

9. Turkey Vulture

The turkey vulture's Latin name (*Cathartes aura*) means "purifier" because it eats dead, decaying animals. Its head resembles a turkey's. Unlike other birds, turkey vultures have a strong sense of smell and are sometimes used to sniff out gas leaks in pipelines.

10. Western Banded Gecko

At night, this desert lizard hunts for insects, spiders, and baby scorpions. It stores extra food as fat in its tail. If a predator steps on the tail and snaps it off, the banded gecko can grow a new one.

The Great Kiva in Chaco Culture National Historical Park was built by the ancient Puebloans.

From the Beginning

2

Long before Europeans set sail for North America, great cultures thrived in the land that is now called New Mexico. In spite of the region's rugged landscape, early peoples in the area lived in harmony with the land, just as present-day New Mexicans live in harmony with the ways of the past.

The Old Ones

Around twelve thousand years ago, New Mexico's first people roamed the grasslands hunting bison, mammoths, mastodons, and antelope. They made tools and weapons out of stone and bone. Eventually, the climate became drier, and many types of large animals died out or migrated to other areas in search of food. So the people—ancestors of today's Native Americans—started a new way of life. They hunted smaller animals and gathered nuts and berries. After a time, they built villages out of dried mud and stone, and they began growing crops such as corn, squash, melons, and beans.

Two of these ancient groups were the Mogollon, who lived in what is now southwestern New Mexico, and the Ancestral Puebloans, who lived in the north. (The Ancestral Puebloans are sometimes referred to as the Anasazi.) The first pottery in the Southwest was made by the Mogollon. They also built round houses that were set partly below ground.

An ancient Mongolon village built more than seven hundred years ago can be visited at Gila Cliff Dwellings National Monument.

Many Ancient Sites

More than twenty-five thousand Anasazi sites have been identified in New Mexico by archeologists. The Anasazi set up an amazing civilization, and they are the ancestors of the Pueblo People. Their great classical period lasted from 1100 to 1300 CE.

The houses faced a central plaza. Each village also included a **kiva**. A kiva is a circular room with a central fireplace used by men and boys for worship or rituals. Usually made of adobe—sun-dried bricks formed from clay, water, and straw or grass—it often can be entered only by a ladder through a hole in the roof. Kivas still exist in ancient ruins throughout New Mexico and are found in many present-day Native American villages as well.

The Mogollon were expert farmers. They traded with the other ancient group, the Ancestral Puebloans. The Ancestral Puebloans were mainly basket makers, hunters and gatherers. But they soon learned farming and pottery-making from the Mogollon. The Ancestral Puebloans used stone and adobe to build extraordinary towns, plazas, kivas, and cliff dwellings. Their largest city was in Chaco Canyon. Chaco was an important site for trading, as well as a cultural and religious center. Hundreds of hand-laid stone roads led into Chaco. Small bands of Ancestral Puebloan families built houses that can still be seen along these roads. These simple villages are called "Chaco outliers."

A Taos photographer once said, "Chaco is simply magical." Today, Chaco Canyon is both a UNESCO World Heritage Site and a national historical park, managed by the US National Park Service. There are thirteen major ruins and more than four hundred smaller archaeological sites in the park.

By around 1300–1400 CE, the Ancestral Puebloan and Mogollon civilizations had mysteriously disappeared. Many scientists believe these ancestral tribes left their villages because water became scarce. They probably joined with other native cultures. Today's Pueblo people, who had established a number of villages in the region by the 1500s, are believed to be their descendants.

Among the spectacular sites left behind by the Ancestral Pueblo People is Bandelier National Monument near Los Alamos. The 33,000-acre (13,350-hectare) monument is located in the southern part of the Pajarito Plateau.

The diversity of life in Frijoles Canyon provided food for people who lived in Alcove House in Bandelier National Monument.

The Native People

When the first Spanish explorers reached the area we now call New Mexico, they encountered many Native American tribes spread out across the territory. These tribes included the Pueblo, Apache, Comanche, Jocome, Jano, Navajo, Ute, and Zuni.

While each of these tribes lived in different regions of the area, spoke different languages, and had different customs, the borders were not rigid and the people shared territory with tribes they were friendly with. The Pueblo people lived along the upper Rio Grande, except for a desert group east of Albuquerque, which lived in the same kind of apartment-like villages as the river Pueblos. During the thirteenth century, the Navajo settled in the Four Corners area to become farmers, sheepherders, and occasional enemies of the Pueblos. The Apache were a more **nomadic** and warlike group who came at about the same time. They were hunters, but did trade for corn with the Pueblos.

In the late sixteenth century, the Spanish arrived looking for wealth and for converts to Catholicism. At first, many of the native tribes accepted these new visitors, but they began to resist as the Spanish forced them to change their traditions and beliefs, to pay taxes, and to work for them. Some Pueblos successfully rebelled in 1680 and expelled the settlers, but the Spanish soon returned and eventually took over the entire area.

Today there are twenty-two federally recognized tribes in New Mexico. Sixteen are considered to be members of the broader Pueblo tribe. The others include the Jicarilla Apache Nation, the Mescalero Apache Tribe, the Ohkay Owingeh, the Navajo Nation, the Ute Mountain Tribe of the Ute Mountain

The Navajo moved into the area that is now New Mexico before the Spanish arrived.

Reservation, and the Zuni Tribe of the Zuni Reservation. Federally recognized tribes have a government-to-government relationship with the United States and are eligible for funding and services from the Bureau of Indian Affairs. They also have certain rights of self-government (i.e., tribal **sovereignty**) and are entitled to receive certain federal benefits, services, and protections because of their special relationship with the United States. Today there are more than 219,000 Native Americans living in New Mexico, making up nearly 11 percent of the population.

Spotlight on the Pueblo

Pueblo is pronounced "PWAY-bloh." This means "town" or "village" in Spanish, and was originally used to refer to the cliff dwellings and large adobe houses where the native peoples lived. Today, the word Pueblo is also used to refer to these tribes themselves.

Distribution: The Pueblo are natives of the Southwest deserts, particularly New Mexico. Unlike many Native American tribes, the Pueblos were never forced to leave their homelands and still live there today.

Homes: Pueblo people lived in multi-story house complexes made of adobe and stone. Pueblo people used ladders to reach the upstairs apartments.

Government: The nineteen Pueblos of New Mexico belong to a confederation which makes joint political decisions on behalf of all. Each Pueblo has its own local government, but the Pueblos are also US citizens and must obey American law.

Clothing: Men wore breechcloths or short kilts and cloth headbands tied around their foreheads. Women wore knee-length cotton dresses called mantas. Both wore deerskin moccasins.

Language: Almost all Pueblo people speak English today, but most also speak one of the native Pueblo languages. Though the Pueblos have closely related cultures, tribes have different names and they do not all speak the same language.

Food: Pueblos raised crops of corn, beans, squash, and sunflowers, as well as cotton and tobacco. Pueblo men hunted while women gathered nuts, fruits, and herbs.

Crafts: Pueblo artists are famous for their beautiful pottery and heishi jewelry. They also make stone carvings, baskets, and colorful weavings.

There is evidence that Native Americans had lived in this region as long as ten thousand years ago. The Ancestral People began building more permanent settlements around 1150 CE. One of these was constructed in Frijoles Canyon.

There were volcanic eruptions 1.6 million years ago and 1.4 million years ago that formed two mountain ranges. The difference in height of these ranges is nearly 5,000 feet (1,524 m), giving this area a diversity of plant and animal life that could sustain the people who lived there.

Frijoles Canyon was formed by erosion in the volcanic **tuff**. Tuff is formed from hot ash that cooled, and it is soft and light. The Ancestral People carved homes in the tuff on the sides of the steep cliffs and built an adobe structure across the entrance to the canyon for housing and maybe protection. They lived in this canyon for about four hundred years. However, drought and barren soil depleted by too many years of farming made it hard to live there. They left by 1550, but Bandelier National Monument remains to mark their place in history.

Stories passed down tell us that the people of Cochiti Pueblo, which is on the Rio Grande, are descendents of the people who left Frijoles Canyon.

Other native groups, such as the Navajo and the Apache, moved south from areas in present-day Canada to what is now New Mexico. In the beginning, these tribes were nomadic. This means that they moved from place to place, following bison herds and hunting for food. When hunting became harder because there were fewer bison, the Navajo and the Apache raided Pueblo villages for food and other supplies. Eventually, the nomadic tribes settled into their own villages and began farming. Today, the country's largest Native American reservation, the Navajo Nation, covers part of northwestern New Mexico as well as parts of Arizona and Utah.

Staying in Place

The Native Pueblo People of the southwest have lived in the same location longer than any other culture in the nation.

The Spanish Enter

Not long after the Navajo and Apache moved into present-day New Mexico, Spanish explorers arrived in the region. They had conquered the native peoples of Mexico and made that area into a Spanish colony. The Spanish then moved north, searching for gold, silver, gems, and other treasures to send to the king of Spain.

Álvar Núñez Cabeza de Vaca crossed New Mexico during his eight-year effort to reach Mexico from Florida.

The first Spaniard who may have set foot in what is now New Mexico was Álvar Núñez Cabeza de Vaca in 1536. He and three companions had been part of a shipwrecked expedition that originally landed in western Florida in 1528. The men spent several years as slaves to Native Americans in what is now Texas. They heard stories from the native people about the Seven Cities of Cíbola, which were cities thought to be so rich that the streets were lined with gold. After escaping from his captors, Cabeza de Vaca made his way through the Southwest and down to Mexico by 1536, and he related these stories to others.

Francisco Vásquez de Coronado, starting from Mexico in 1540, ventured hundreds of miles into the Great Plains in search of the Seven Cities of Cíbola. He did not find them (they did not exist) and reported the results of his mission to the king of Spain. He wrote, "[It] troubled me greatly to find myself on these limitless plains, where I was in great need of water, and often had to drink it so poor that it was more mud than water." But the lure of riches sent more Spaniards north from Mexico on El Camino Real, "the royal road," into the land they called New Mexico. As Spanish soldiers, settlers, explorers, and priests came upon native villages with buildings made of mud, they called them pueblos after

Making a Pueblo Model

Pueblo Native Americans were known for their mud-brick houses. It's easy to build a Pueblo house (or even a village!).

What You Need

Cardboard boxes in various sizes

Safety scissors

Toilet paper

Bar of soap

Cheese grater

Brown craft paint

Craft sticks

Glue

Tape

What You Do

- Draw square windows and doors onto cardboard boxes. Use safety scissors to cut out the holes. Tape or glue the boxes together, with the windows on the same side. The shorter boxes go in front.

- Place small bits of toilet paper into a large bowl. Grate the bar of soap into the bowl using the cheese grater. Add warm water a little at a time. Mix the toilet paper, soap, and water together by hand until it feels like thick whipped cream.

- Add a small amount of brown, non-toxic craft paint to the bowl to give the mud its brown color. Use your fingers to mix the mud and spread it all over your cardboard boxes. Be sure to cover every side.

- Let the pueblo dry overnight. If necessary, touch it up with brown craft paint after the mud has dried.

- Glue craft sticks together to form ladders. Set up ladders between different levels.

the Spanish word for "town." The Native Americans living in these villages also became known as Pueblos.

When the Spanish came across a Pueblo village, they assigned it a patron saint. A patron saint guides or protects a person or a place. Today, there are nineteen traditional Pueblo villages in New Mexico. Some of them have kept their Spanish saint names, such as Santa Clara, San Felipe, San Juan, Santa Ana, and San Ildefonso.

The Spanish had two reasons for exploring the region. One was finding treasure, and the other was spreading the Roman Catholic faith. At first, the native people were friendly toward the newcomers, but the Spanish proved to be terrifying. The Native Americans had never seen men on horseback. Some were frightened by the gleaming swords the Spanish carried as weapons and by the violence of the newcomers.

The first Spanish settlement in New Mexico was near the Rio Grande, north of present-day Santa Fe. In 1598, four hundred settlers led by Don Juan de Oñate established haciendas, or ranches. The settlers found it difficult to farm the dry land and forced the native peoples living in the area to work the fields. Oñate built Catholic missions throughout the region, and priests tried to make the Pueblos practice Christianity. The Spanish burned kivas, destroyed sacred objects, and challenged the Pueblos' religious

The Quarai Mission complex includes one of four mission churches built in the 1600s that are among the sites in Salinas Pueblo Missions National Monument.

leaders. Oñate's soldiers were so brutal that he was eventually sent back to Mexico City in disgrace. Spain wanted to abandon New Mexico completely, but the priests refused to leave behind the Native Americans who had become Christians. So Spain declared that New Mexico would be missionary land.

Then, in 1609, a new Spanish governor arrived, Don Pedro de Peralta. He established a new capital city and named it Santa Fe. Despite the new leader, the relationship between the Spanish and the Pueblos did not improve. The native peoples resented working on the haciendas, tending the mission gardens, wearing European clothing, and being forced to accept a religion other than their own.

By 1680, the Pueblo people had had enough. A religious leader named Popé led the most successful revolt by native peoples in the New World, an event that became known as the Pueblo Revolt. Pueblo leaders sent runners as messengers to the many nearby Native American communities to inform them of the planned revolt. Every community leader received a knotted rope. Each day, the leaders untied a knot. When all the knots were gone, the Native Americans knew it was time to fight. They surrounded the Spanish settlements and forced the Spanish to withdraw. When the Spanish returned in 1692, led by Don Diego de Vargas, they allowed the Pueblos to practice their ancestral religion along with Christianity. Spain continued to control New Mexico for more than one hundred more years.

Biggest Fire

The largest fire in New Mexico's history started at Bandelier National Monument on May 4, 2000, when a controlled burn meant to clear away dry brush and prevent future fires leaped out of control due to high winds. Twenty-five thousand people, including all the residents of Los Alamos, were forced to evacuate their homes.

Mexican Province and US Territory

When Mexico gained its independence from Spain in 1821, New Mexico became a province of Mexico. The Mexican rulers were much more interested in trade with the United States than the Spanish had been. American traders established the Santa Fe Trail, which opened up the Southwest to American interests. The Trail ran from Missouri to Santa Fe and helped traders bring many goods to New Mexico. These included clothing, candles, books, furniture, and knives. In exchange, New Mexicans sent furs and silver eastward on the trail.

The Santa Fe Trail allowed wagon trains to reach New Mexico before the railroad was built.

The Santa Fe Trail was the first of the great trails that expanded American settlement westward. The trail remained a major trade route until 1880, when the Santa Fe Railroad was completed.

In 1846, the United States and Mexico went to war. A US general named Stephen Kearny led his troops into New Mexico and took over the province. The war ended two years later. The United States and Mexico signed a treaty that made most of present-day New Mexico part of the United States. The document was called the Treaty of Guadalupe Hidalgo. Several years later, in the Gadsden Purchase of 1853, the United States bought an additional strip of land from Mexico in what is now southern New Mexico and Arizona.

In 1850, Congress established the Territory of New Mexico. The region had a territorial government but was not yet a state. When the Civil War began in 1861, both the Union and the Confederate governments wanted the New Mexico territory on their side. Union and Confederate forces met and fought in the territory in 1862, at the Battle of Glorieta Pass. The Union victory in that battle essentially ended any Confederate threat to US control of New Mexico.

In the mid-1800s, Americans of northern European descent, known as Anglo-Americans or Anglos, moved into New Mexico. They came to find new homes, adventure, and gold. Warrior tribes, such as the Apache, Comanche, Kiowa, and Navajo, were bitter about the Anglos invading their lands. Bloody fighting took place over several decades

10 KEY CITIES

Albuquerque

Roswell

1. Albuquerque: population 545,852

New Mexico's largest city, Albuquerque has been shaped by centuries of history. Now a center of high-tech industry, research, and culture, Albuquerque retains vital connections to the past, such as the ancient rock carvings at Petroglyph National Monument.

2. Las Cruces: population 97,618

Located in the Mesilla Valley, Las Cruces was founded in 1849 at a major crossroads for travel routes in the state. New Mexico State University's main campus is located here and Prehistoric Trackways National Monument is nearby.

3. Rio Rancho: population 87,521

New Mexico's fastest growing city, Rio Rancho offers a mild, high desert climate perfect for outdoor adventures year-round. Located in Sandoval County, the city is fifteen minutes from Albuquerque and offers a variety of landscapes.

4. Santa Fe: population 67,947

New Mexico's state capital, Santa Fe is also its oldest city and the oldest state capital in the United States. It is famous as a center of arts, culture, and science. Los Alamos and Sandia National Laboratories are located nearby.

5. Roswell: population 48,366

Located in southeastern New Mexico, Roswell is a city full of mystery and wonder. Roswell offers many activities and attractions but is perhaps best known for the Roswell UFO Museum & Research Center.

NEW MEXICO ★ ★

6. Farmington: population 45,877

Farmington serves as a great destination for history buffs and nature lovers. Close to the Four Corners, the region offers access to Native American history, national parks, World Heritage Sites, and events like amateur baseball's Connie Mack World Series.

7. Clovis: population 37,775

Clovis is located in southeastern New Mexico just nine miles from the Texas border. While known mainly for agriculture and ranching, Clovis also supports Cannon Air Force base, part of the Air Force Special Operations Command.

8. Hobbs: population 34,122

Hobbs is the largest municipality in Lea County, the southeastern-most county of New Mexico's thirty-three counties. The Hobbs area includes Native American legacy, cowboy legend, farming traditions, and Hispanic culture, all enshrined in its museums and libraries.

9. Alamogordo: population 30,403

Settled as a rail junction in 1898, Alamogordo is now a thriving community connected to nearby Holloman Air Force Base and White Sands Missile Range. Alamogordo also serves as a gateway to White Sands National Monument.

10. Carlsbad: population 26,138

Carlsbad is located in the Chihuahuan Desert on the Pecos River. The city, with a greenway along Lake Carlsbad, originated as an oasis, "The Pearl on the Pecos." Carlsbad Caverns National Park is located nearby.

Four Corners
near Farmington

Carlsbad

This general store was built on an Apache reservation just south of Ruidoso.

between US soldiers and Native Americans, including Apache groups led by warriors such as Geronimo and Cochise.

In the 1860s, the US government sent Kit Carson to round up Navajo groups and force them onto a reservation in eastern New Mexico. Carson was a trapper and a scout who had friends among the Native American tribes. Still, he followed government orders and in 1864 forced thousands of Navajos to walk 300 miles (485 km) across wintry northern New Mexico to a reservation on the eastern plains. Hundreds died during this tragic march, which became known as the Long Walk.

The Navajos were allowed to return to their traditional homelands in 1868, after agreeing to a new peace treaty with the United States government. The Navajos were an exception in terms of keeping their homelands. Most other native groups were slowly moved away from their traditional homelands. The last of the wars against Native Americans in New Mexico ended when Geronimo and his band surrendered in 1886.

By the time the Anglos came to New Mexico in large numbers, the area's Pueblo groups and Hispanic settlers had inhabited New Mexico together for more than two hundred years. As farmers and ranchers, they had banded together for protection from the raids of other tribes. They had intermarried to some degree and had also, to some

Historical Palace

The Palace of Governors in Santa Fe, built in 1610, is one of the oldest public buildings in North America.

extent, learned to share and accept each other's culture. But the Anglos brought a new culture and way of life. After the Civil War, Anglos took over the territorial government and achieved positions of power in many New Mexican communities.

The "New" New Mexico

In the second half of the nineteenth century, the New Mexico Territory became part of the lively American West. The territory filled with cowboys, railroad workers, miners, gunfighters, gamblers, and adventurers. Cattle ranching became big business as new railroads made it easier to transport cattle to eastern markets. But the sudden growth led to conflicts. Cattle ranches needed water, and landowners argued over water rights.

In Lincoln County, a feud in 1878 between cattle ranchers turned into a bloody war. One local gunfighter became a legend. Born as William Henry McCarty and also using the name William Bonney, this outlaw was more famously known by his nickname Billy the Kid. He was hired to protect one of the ranchers, who was then murdered. When the war was settled by Governor Lew Wallace, after nineteen people died, Billy the Kid was still wanted. He was eventually killed in 1881. He was celebrated in poems, songs, and even a symphony.

As early as 1850, New Mexicans asked Congress to make New Mexico a US state. But many members of Congress were unsure. Some did not trust New Mexicans, most of whom were either Hispanic or Native American, and did not like the fact that the primary language of many New Mexicans was Spanish. So Congress did not approve statehood, and the New Mexico Territory was created instead.

Distrust of New Mexicans arose again in 1898 during the Spanish-American War. Some people in the eastern United States believed that New Mexico's large Hispanic population would cause it to side with Spain in the war. President William McKinley nevertheless asked New Mexico's territorial governor to send volunteers to help the war effort. The response was overwhelming. Future president Theodore

Billy the Kid

Roosevelt welcomed many New Mexican soldiers into the Rough Riders. This volunteer cavalry unit led by Roosevelt helped to free the island of Cuba from Spanish rule. Finally, on January 6, 1912, New Mexico was granted statehood, becoming the forty-seventh US state.

Changes Big and Small

In the early 1900s, doctors in the East started sending patients to New Mexico for the warm weather and the clean, dry air. Artists, writers, photographers, and tourists came as well and were struck by the region's beauty. In a letter from Santa Fe, the photographer Ansel Adams wrote, "This is a place to work—and dream."

The beauty of the area sometimes led to problems for the Native Americans. For example, in 1906 an area called Blue Lake was taken over by the government and eventually made part of Carson National Forest. The takeover was directed by an Executive Order of President Theodore Roosevelt, and the lake was put under the control of the US Forest Service.

People who lived in the area were unhappy. The people of the Taos Pueblo considered Blue Lake a sacred shrine. They believed it was the place of their origin. Severino Martinez, who was governor of the Taos Pueblo in the mid 1950s, called Blue Lake "our Indian church."

The brilliant colors of Kitchen Mesa near Abiquiu are highlighted by the sharp angle of the sun.

The Taos Pueblo relies on water that comes from the Blue Lake watershed.

The lake is also the source of a river that runs through the pueblo, providing clean drinking water for its residents and their animals. The people of the pueblo immediately began trying to regain control of the 48,000 acre (19,425 ha) Blue Lake watershed.

The Forest Service wanted to keep control of the land so lumber could be harvested and people could go hunting, fishing, and camping there. There were four hearings in Congress from 1966 to 1970 over who should have control over the land. Many bills written to restore the land to the people of the Taos Pueblo had failed in Congress, but support for the Native American cause was building.

The movement eventually gained the support of President Richard Nixon and his administration. Congress finally passed a bill returning control of the area to its rightful owners, and President Nixon signed it into law on December 15, 1970.

President Nixon stated, "This is a bill that represents justice, because in 1906 an injustice was done in which land involved in this bill, 48,000 acres (19,425 ha), was taken from the Taos Pueblo Native Americans. The Congress of the United States now returns that land to whom it belongs … I can't think of anything more appropriate that could make

The Santa Rita Mine, which yields copper, is one of the oldest continuously operating mines in the West.

me more proud as President of the United States." In 2010, a celebration was held in Taos Pueblo to mark the fortieth anniversary of the return of Blue Lake to the Ancestral People.

While many people came to New Mexico early in the twentieth century for the area's healthful climate and natural beauty, others came to make a living off the land. Mining companies dug for copper, silver, lead, gold, and other minerals. Energy companies drilled for oil and natural gas. In remote areas, the US military established a number of airfields, military outposts, and research laboratories.

One of those remote areas was located at White Sands National Monument. In 1942, a few months after the attack by Japan on Pearl Harbor, President Franklin D. Roosevelt created the Alamogordo Bombing and Gunnery Range. It covered 1,243,000 acres (503,024 ha). The order allowed soldiers to practice tank maneuvers inside the park. The military began to test missiles by 1945 and asked for the first park closures, a practice that continues today. White Sands Missile Range is still in use.

New Mexicans and the Military

New Mexicans have long been active in the US military. When the United States entered World War I in 1917, the newly admitted state

An Old Way of Speaking

In some isolated villages, such as Truchas, Chimayo, and Coyote in north-central New Mexico, some descendants of Spanish conquistadors still speak a form of sixteenth century Spanish used nowhere else in the world today.

contributed troops to the US forces fighting in Europe. The state offered even more troops when the United States fought in World War II from 1941 to 1945.

One noteworthy World War II unit was the Navajo code talkers, members of the US Marine Corps. From 1942 to 1945, these highly trained soldiers used a code based on their native language to deliver secret messages to US soldiers on the battlefields in the Pacific, fighting against Japan. The Navajo soldiers were chosen because their language is unique and difficult to translate. At the time, fewer than thirty people who were non-Navajos could speak the language. The Japanese military included skilled code-breakers, but they never broke the Navajo code.

For many years, the American public did not know about the participation of the Navajo code talkers in World War II. The Marines continued to use the code based on the Navajo language after the war and therefore could not discuss it openly. In 1992, the code talkers were honored at the Pentagon (the US Defense Department headquarters near Washington, DC) for their contributions to their country.

The Manhattan Project

The Manhattan Project was another World War II military program in which New Mexico played a major part. The purpose of the project was to secretly develop the first atomic bomb. This weapon is a powerful bomb that gets its force from the energy given off

Navajo code talkers gave the United States a big advantage in World War II because the Japanese couldn't break their code.

from splitting atoms—the building blocks of all matter. One of the chief scientists on the project was Robert Oppenheimer, who had camped as a child in the remote mountains of northern New Mexico, near the village of Los Alamos. He suggested that the project's main laboratory should be hidden there.

When it was time to test a bomb, scientists chose a remote site named Trinity, near the town of Alamogordo. In 1945, they placed the first atomic bomb on a steel tower erected in the desert. On July 16, when they exploded the bomb, it broke windows in houses as far as 120 miles (195 km)

The atomic bomb was tested near Alamogordo.

away. Weeks later, the United States dropped similar bombs on the Japanese cities of Hiroshima and Nagasaki, which led almost immediately to the end of World War II.

In the second half of the twentieth century and the beginning of the twenty-first, people continued to move to New Mexico to live, work, and enjoy the lifestyle and natural beauty. In 1950, fewer than seven hundred thousand people lived in the state. By 1970, the number of residents had passed one million, and by 2010, more than two million people called New Mexico home. Some of the newer residents came to work in mining, in government laboratories, in agriculture, and in the oil and natural gas industries. Artists and retirees have also come to New Mexico in large numbers.

In Their Own Words

"New Mexico is full of brave men and women who have dedicated their lives to service."
—US Senator Tom Udall

A lifelong resident of Las Cruces has remarked, "People just trickle in on the interstate. First they leave California, and then they find Phoenix, Scottsdale, Tucson, and here. But when they get here, they stay." After looking at New Mexico's colorful past, it is easy to understand why people fought for the right to stay, to live, and to work in this extraordinary land.

10 KEY DATES IN NEW MEXICO HISTORY

1. 1-1300 CE

The Ancestral Puebloans, living as hunter-gatherers, establish permanent settlements and build elaborate stone and adobe structures known as pueblos.

2. April 30, 1598

Don Juan de Oñate brings colonists to northern New Mexico and issues a declaration claiming the territory as a Spanish possession, Nuevo Mexico.

3. August 10, 1680

After suffering suppression from the Spanish for many years, Pueblo leader Popé organizes a revolt, forcing the Spanish settlers to leave the region.

4. September 27, 1821

Mexico wins independence from Spain, ending nearly three centuries of Spanish rule and making New Mexico a part of the Mexican Republic.

5. February 2, 1848

Mexico surrenders present-day New Mexico, California, and Arizona, parts of Utah, Nevada, Colorado, and claims to Texas to the United States in the treaty ending the Mexican-American War.

6. January 1864

Thousands of Native Americans are forced to march hundreds of miles to a reservation in eastern New Mexico. Hundreds of people die during the journey, known as the Long Walk.

7. September 4, 1886

Apache leader Geronimo surrenders, ending the last Native American war in the region. He had battled for thirty years to protect his tribe's homeland.

8. January 6, 1912

New Mexico becomes the forty-seventh state. After the defeat of New Mexico's Native Americans, the population of New Mexico grows rapidly.

9. July 16, 1945

The first atomic bomb was tested in an isolated area of the New Mexico desert at the Trinity site near Alamogordo.

10. January 1, 2011

Susana Martinez is sworn in as New Mexico's first female governor. She is also the first Hispanic female governor in the United States.

The Dineh Tah Navajo Dancers perform in Santa Fe.

The People

3

New Mexican society is based largely on three cultures: Native American, Hispanic, and Anglo. Through the centuries, these groups of very different people have sometimes disagreed. Yet over time, they have grown to share each other's customs and traditions. Today, the numbers of Asian Americans and African Americans are increasing in the state. However, African Americans represent only about 2 percent of the population, and Asian Americans a little more than 1 percent. The three primary cultures have played the largest part in shaping the state so far.

Regardless of their racial, ethnic, and cultural backgrounds, New Mexicans are proud of their communities, which are rich with diversity and heritage.

The Native People

Native Americans make up more than 10 percent of the population of New Mexico. Many of these people maintain close ties to their ancestral lands and traditions. The state's three major Native American groups are the Pueblo, Apache, and Navajo.

The Pueblo people share a similar culture, but they do not all speak the same Native language. Of the Pueblo villages established centuries ago, nineteen remain active communities. The people of each Pueblo village have a distinct artistic or craft tradition or means of making a living. For example, a number of people living in the Santa Clara, San Ildefonso, and Acoma pueblos are potters. Many of the Isleta Pueblo residents are farmers. Many people in the Picuris Pueblo are painters. Jewelry making is a common craft in the Santo Domingo and Zuni pueblos. Today, not all Pueblo people live in their ancient villages. Many live in nearby towns or cities. But even for them, it is important to visit the Pueblo villages for celebrations and feast days.

The Navajo create beautiful rugs.

The Apache and the Navajo also add to the state's blend of native cultures. Today, many Apaches, although not all, live on reservations. The Jicarilla Apache reservation is in northern New Mexico, and the Mescalero reservation is in the south. Many Apaches work for tribal-owned ranches, resorts, and mining operations.

The Navajo Nation covers 16 million acres (6.5 million ha) in the Four Corners region. Much of the reservation lies in Arizona and Utah, but about one-third of the Navajos live in New Mexico. The town of Shiprock, New Mexico, with about 8,300 residents, is an urban center within the reservation boundaries. Navajos hold a variety of jobs, but many are weavers, silversmiths, farmers, and sheepherders. On the reservation, visitors can see Navajo **hogans**. These are traditional buildings that are usually round or multi-sided. They are made of logs and are sometimes covered with earth. Although only a few families in remote areas still live in hogans, many extended families, or clans, have one for special ceremonies.

The Hispanic Tradition

Before any English colonies had been established in what is now the eastern United States, the Spanish had formed settlements in New Mexico. Spanish families in the Southwest have lived longer in the present-day United States than the descendants of the first English settlers in Virginia and New England.

In colonial times, Spanish rulers gave their nobles large land grants in Mexico and New Mexico. Landowners learned how to farm from the Pueblos and established farms as well as sheep ranches. Most of the settlers grew what they needed and traded for what they did not produce themselves. Albuquerque, founded in 1706, became an important trading center. The Spanish also first brought to New Mexico the Catholic faith, which is still practiced by many people throughout the state.

Today, about 46 percent of New Mexico's population is Hispanic. Some New Mexicans can trace their origins back to the noble families who were granted land by the Spanish rulers. Others are the descendants of Hispanic people who arrived later in New Mexico's history. Many of the state's new residents are immigrants from Mexico. Overall, more than 60 percent of Hispanics in New Mexico are of Mexican heritage. About one out of three New Mexican families speaks Spanish at home.

Through the years, New Mexican culture has been influenced deeply by Spanish traditions and language. Across the state, there are businesses, communities, and events that share and celebrate the state's Spanish heritage.

Rodeos give cowboys from diverse backgrounds a chance to show their skills.

The Anglos

More than two-thirds of New Mexico's population is white. These people include descendants of the Anglos who made their way to New Mexico in the nineteenth century. Showing spirit and courage, they came as miners, cowboys, ranchers, and adventurers. Today, New Mexico's white population includes new arrivals and the descendants of many people who chose the state as their home in the twentieth century and early years of the twenty-first—drawn to the state by climate, job opportunities, or the appealing lifestyle.

★ 10 ★ KEY PEOPLE ★ ★

Jeff Bezos

Jesse Tyler Ferguson

Geronimo

1. Jeff Bezos

Jeff Bezos was born in Albuquerque in 1964. After studying computer science in college, he became vice president of a large financial company. He left his job and started Amazon.com after noticing the dramatic growth of the Internet.

2. John Denver

Singer/songwriter John Denver was born in 1943 in Roswell. He wrote and performed many hit songs, including "Rocky Mountain High." He died in a plane crash in 1997.

3. Jesse Tyler Ferguson

Jesse Tyler Ferguson is best known for portraying Mitchell Pritchett on the ABC sitcom *Modern Family*. Born in Montana on October 22, 1975, he and his family moved to Albuquerque where, at age eight, he joined the Albuquerque Children's Theater.

4. Arian Foster

Born in Albuquerque in 1986, Arian Foster became a running back for the National Football League's Houston Texans. In 2010, Foster led the NFL in rushing and touchdowns. Foster played college football at the University of Tennessee.

5. Geronimo

Born in New Mexico in 1829, Geronimo swore revenge after his wife and children were killed in a Mexican army raid. Geronimo fought for decades against US and Mexican armies. In 1886, he became the last Native American leader to surrender.

6. William Hanna

William Hanna was born in Melrose in 1910. He loved to draw and moved to Hollywood, partnering with Joseph Barbera to form Hanna-Barbera. Their cartoon characters include Yogi Bear, Scooby Doo, and the Flintstones.

7. Neil Patrick Harris

Born in Albuquerque in 1973, Neil Patrick Harris began acting at an early age. He has starred in television series (including *Doogie Howser, M.D.* and *How I Met Your Mother*), and is also famous for his stage and film work.

8. Nancy Lopez

Nancy Lopez was born in California but moved to Roswell as a child. At twelve, Nancy won the state amateur golf championship. She then won forty-eight professional tournaments and became the youngest golfer ever admitted to the Ladies Professional Golf Association (LPGA) Hall of Fame.

9. Demi Lovato

Demetria (Demi) Devonne Lovato was born in 1992 in Albuquerque. She began performing at an early age, starring in children's television shows and the Disney Channel movie *Camp Rock*. Demi also sings and performs at concerts.

10. Georgia O'Keeffe

Georgia O'Keeffe was born in 1887 in Wisconsin but later moved to Ghost Ranch, near Abiquiu. Her paintings feature desert flowers, adobe churches, and animal skeletons. She is considered one of the best American Modernist painters.

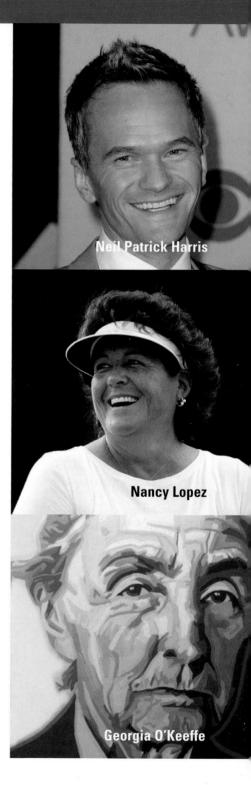

Neil Patrick Harris

Nancy Lopez

Georgia O'Keeffe

Who New Mexicans Are

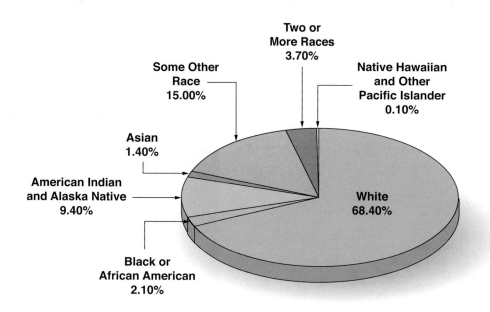

Two or More Races
3.70%

Some Other Race
15.00%

Native Hawaiian and Other Pacific Islander
0.10%

Asian
1.40%

American Indian and Alaska Native
9.40%

White
68.40%

Black or African American
2.10%

Total Population
2,059,179

Hispanic or Latino (of any race):

• **953,403 people (46.3%)**

Note: The pie chart shows the racial breakdown of the state's population based on the categories used by the U.S. Bureau of the Census. The Census Bureau reports information for Hispanics or Latinos separately, since they may be of any race. Percentages in the pie chart may not add to 100 because of rounding.

Source: US Bureau of the Census, 2010 Census

The Arts

New Mexicans are proud that their state is nationally recognized as a center for the arts. Nature and tradition often inspire New Mexican artists. For example, the people of the Santa Clara Pueblo feel that they are part of the land. They use the same word—nung—to mean both people and clay. Pottery objects made in pueblos such as Cochiti, Santa Clara, Acoma, and San Ildefonso are collected by museums around the world.

Native American jewelry makers are known for their fine work in silver and turquoise. Navajos use wool from their sheep to create highly prized rugs and blankets. The Apache are known for their elegant handmade baskets. Traditionally, New Mexico's Native Americans painted with sand or on rock. Today, many blend old ways with modern styles to create unique works.

In the early part of the twentieth century, Anglo artists from distant places such as New York and Europe visited Taos and Santa Fe. There, they painted the striking landscape. The best known was Georgia O'Keeffe, who observed, "All the earth colors of the painter's palette are

In Their Own Words

"I was born on the prairies where the wind blew free and there was nothing to break the light of the sun. I was born where there were no enclosures." —Geronimo

Santa Fe is a destination for art lovers.

out there in the many miles of badlands …" Today, hundreds of art galleries display artwork in these New Mexican cities. In Santa Fe alone, more than a dozen museums thrive.

Santa Fe, Center for the Arts

The United Nations Educational, Scientific, and Cultural Organization (UNESCO) has endorsed Santa Fe as a member of the Creative Cities Network. Member cities worldwide cooperate in promoting the arts and encouraging cultural diversity. Santa Fe qualified in the Crafts and Folk Art category.

In architecture, Spanish and Pueblo designs are combined to create what is called Santa Fe style. It features buildings constructed out of earth-colored adobe. Wood timbers, called vigas, form the framework and poke through the adobe. On the inside, an adobe fireplace is often located in the corner of the living room, and bold Navajo rugs cover clay tile floors. These buildings are both attractive and practical. The adobe and tile keep the houses cool in summer and warm in winter.

Great Food

New Mexico has a state question: "Red or green?" What it means is, "What color chiles would you like on your food?" New Mexico is one of the few states in the United States with a regional cuisine, or way of cooking. Using chiles, corn, beans, and squash as basic ingredients, New Mexican–style cooking has become world famous.

Music has also been a strong part of New Mexican culture. Music lovers from around the world gather under the stars at the open-air Santa Fe Opera House to listen to classical music. Native Americans use music in their ceremonies and celebrations. One well-known symbol of New Mexico is the humpbacked, flute-playing Native American god Kokopelli, who serves his people as a magician, musician, rain priest, healer, prankster, and song carrier. The Spaniards and Mexicans brought mariachi music to the state. Anglos brought European folk songs and cowboy ballads.

Education and Sports

Excellence in education has long been a priority in New Mexico. From kindergarten through high school, more than 330,000 students attend some 860 public schools across the state. However, some rural schools suffer from inadequate financial support.

The University of New Mexico and New Mexico State University are the leading public universities in the state. The University of New Mexico's main campus is in Albuquerque, and the State University's is in Las Cruces. Each university has four satellite campuses around the state. Other public universities include the New Mexico Institute of Mining and Technology, Eastern New Mexico University, and Western New Mexico University.

There are also several private colleges and universities in New Mexico. Included among these is St. John's College in Santa Fe, which is nationally known for its creative approach to higher education.

There are no major professional sports teams in New Mexico. However, many fans root for the Lobos, the University of New Mexico teams, and the Aggies, the teams representing New Mexico State University.

Many Forms of Faith

The British novelist D. H. Lawrence said the religion of New Mexico's Native Americans was "a vast old religion, greater than anything …" The spiritual life of many Native Americans is tied closely to nature. They celebrate their faith in kivas, in dances, and at festivals honoring the natural world. The Navajo have a ritual called the Blessing Way. A singer performs to remove evil or fear, to protect people and animals, or to ask for an agreeable life. Sometimes, a Blessing Way song can last for several days.

The adobe San Francisco de Asís church was built more than two hundred years ago.

When the Spanish arrived and converted many of the Pueblos to Catholicism, the Native Americans kept many of their rituals, but they added elements of the Catholic faith. For example, traditional dances such as the Corn Dance or Deer Dance are now held on a Christian saint's day.

As Spanish priests spread their religion throughout New Mexico, they also built churches and missions that are noteworthy works of architecture. Many of these beautiful historic buildings feature adobe walls, folk paintings, elaborate carvings, and white crosses that stand out against the deep blue sky.

People of other religions have also found a home in New Mexico. Mormon temples, Protestant churches, Jewish temples, and Hindu temples contribute to the religious diversity of the state. The country's only adobe Islamic mosque is located in Abiquiu.

Issues for the Future

New Mexico is not a wealthy state in terms of income (the money that is made through work). There are jobs in the cities, but not enough for everyone. In the past, many Hispanics and Native Americans were farmers and ranchers. Those skills are needed less in today's economy. About one in five New Mexicans now lives in poverty.

In recent decades, wealthy newcomers have moved to cities such as Taos, Santa Fe, and Las Cruces to purchase or build vacation or retirement homes. Prices for land and housing increased in these areas, reaching levels many long-time residents found difficult to afford. The cost of housing did drop in 2008 and subsequent years as the US economy went through a recession. However, the gap between what different groups of New Mexicans can afford is a problem that causes friction.

But New Mexico has a long multicultural history. New Mexicans know how to blend many ways of life to build a society that tries to represent everyone. Former US congressman Steve Schiff has stated, "Despite some differences, New Mexicans on the whole deal with racial and ethnic diversity much better than the rest of the country." Jeff Bingaman, a US senator from New Mexico from 1983 to 2013, thinks so too. He has affirmed, "I think most New Mexicans would agree … our state is a shining example of what's right."

10 KEY EVENTS ★ ★ ★

Albuquerque International Balloon Festival

1. Albuquerque International Balloon Festival

For ten days every October, one of the world's largest hot-air balloon and gas balloon events takes place. Hundreds of thousands of people watch more than six hundred colorful balloons float in New Mexico's blue skies.

2. Clovis Pioneer Days

Every June in the eastern New Mexican city of Clovis, people enjoy parades, rodeos, quilt shows, and the Miss Rodeo New Mexico Pageant. The event celebrates farming and ranching.

3. Festival of the Cranes

Each November during their migration, sandhill cranes stop at the Bosque del Apache National Wildlife Refuge, near the city of Socorro. New Mexicans celebrate the return of the cranes and other wildlife with arts and crafts, workshops, exhibits, and of course, bird-watching.

Gathering of Nations Powwow

4. Fiesta de Santa Fe

Late August brings the nation's oldest celebration, the Fiesta de Santa Fe. This event marks the peaceful Spanish reconquest of New Mexico after the Pueblo Revolt of 1680. The festival includes music, a crafts market, a pet parade, and the Historical/Hysterical Parade.

5. Gathering of Nations Powwow

Each April in Albuquerque, representatives from five hundred US and Canadian Native American tribes come together to share their cultures. Activities include dancing and the Indian Traders Market, which has Native American art, artifacts, traditional foods, and other items.

NEW MEXICO ★ ★ ★

6. Hatch Chile Festival

The little town of Hatch is known as the green chile capital of the world. The town's population more than doubles during the chile harvest, held over Labor Day weekend. Lovers of spicy foods come to taste the latest chile crop.

7. New Mexico State Fair

The New Mexico State Fair is a harvest festival overflowing with ethnic foods, entertainment, arts and crafts, animal exhibits, a rodeo, concerts, and more. Held in Albuquerque each September, the fair has something for everyone.

8. Roswell UFO Festival

Thousands of science fiction fans come to Roswell for its annual festival, marking the day in July 1947 when many believe an alien spacecraft crashed in a farmer's field. Roswell is home to the International UFO (Unidentified Flying Object) Museum.

9. Tour of the Gila Bicycle Race

In May, racers from around the world come to the high, rugged Gila Wilderness to test their mountain biking skills. Cyclists compete in a variety of races, including some that span several days and cover hundreds of miles.

10. The Whole Enchilada Fiesta

Held each September in Las Cruces, the fiesta's highlight event is the cooking of The World's Largest Enchilada (The Whole Enchilada), which is listed in the 2000 *Guinness Book of World Records* as the largest, flat, three-layer enchilada.

Hatch Chile Festival

Roswell UFO Festival

Important decisions were made in the Palace of Governors in Santa Fe for almost three hundred years.

How the Government Works

4

For more than three centuries, New Mexico had governors appointed by others—Spain, Mexico, and Washington, DC. Not until New Mexico gained statehood in 1912 were New Mexicans able to elect their own governor and other state government officials.

New Mexico, the State

New Mexico's State Constitution was drafted in 1911 and was put to use the next year. The constitution describes the structure, the powers, and the limits on the power of state government. Many provisions in the constitution are similar to those in the US Constitution, including a bill of rights. But unlike the federal constitution, the New Mexico document includes a provision making both English and Spanish the official state languages.

The Palace of the Governors in Santa Fe housed governors for nearly three hundred years. Today, the state government uses a new State Capitol building called the Roundhouse, which is round and designed to look like a kiva. The Roundhouse has four entrances that stand for the four winds, the four seasons, the four directions, and the four stages of life: infancy, youth, adulthood, and old age. The Palace of the Governors now houses the New Mexico History Museum.

The new state capitol was designed to resemble a kiva.

There are three levels of government in New Mexico: county, municipal, and state. New Mexico has thirty-three counties. People elect commissioners to run county government. Across the state there are 104 cities, towns, or villages. These are called municipalities. People living in these areas elect councils and sometimes mayors to run their local governments. They meet with these lawmakers to discuss issues in town meetings.

Branches of Government

Executive

In the executive branch, the governor, lieutenant governor, secretary of state, and other officials are elected to four-year terms. The governor is the head of the state. His or her duties include preparing the state budget (which the state legislature must approve), suggesting new laws, and choosing cabinet members and other department heads. Those people carry out state laws in a certain area of responsibility, such as education or transportation. The governor also signs into law or rejects bills passed by the legislature. A governor is limited to serving two consecutive four-year terms.

Legislative

The legislative branch, or state legislature, is responsible for passing state laws. It is made up of two houses, or chambers. The Senate has forty-two members, and the House of Representatives has seventy members. Each citizen can vote for one senator and one representative. Senators are elected to four-year terms, and Representatives serve for two years. There is no limit on the number of terms that a member of the legislature can serve.

Judicial

The judicial branch is a system of courts that includes the state Supreme Court, the Court of Appeals, district courts, magistrate courts, and municipal or county courts. Magistrate, municipal, and county courts generally deal with cases involving small amounts of money, minor criminal offenses, or other criminal cases that often do not go to trial. Most criminal and other trials in major cases are held in district courts. Many district court decisions can be appealed to the Court of Appeals, which reviews and can change decisions. Decisions in the most serious criminal cases and certain other types of major cases can be appealed to the Supreme Court. The highest court in the state, the Supreme Court also oversees the functioning of the other courts.

In Their Own Words

"I'm proud of the fact that we were able to work together—the Legislature and the Governor—Democrats and Republicans. We came together and found a better way."
—Governor Susana Martinez on ending the state's budget deficit

Nations within a Nation

New Mexico also has tribal governments that are viewed as separate nations. Each of the nineteen pueblos, the two Apache reservations, and the Navajo Nation has an independent

Tribal governments make decisions for sovereign nations, such as the Navajo Nation.

government. Each government includes an elected tribal council. The head of a Pueblo government is called a governor. The Apache reservations and the Navajo Nation each elect an official called a president to head their governments. Tribal governments have their own constitutions and can collect taxes, as well as pass laws and issue regulations concerning matters ranging from hunting rules to religion. The Navajo Nation has two levels in its court system. There are trial courts and the Supreme Court. Three appellate judges sit on the Supreme Court, including the Chief Justice. Navajo Nation courts hear more than fifty thousand cases each year. Pueblos also have an all-Native American Pueblo Council, which deals with issues affecting all the pueblos, including education and environmental concerns.

All Native Americans in New Mexico may now also vote in state, local, and federal elections. The state constitution barred them from voting until a federal court ruled in 1948 that the state constitution conflicted with the US Constitution and federal law.

How a Bill Becomes a Law

In New Mexico, state lawmakers introduce new bills every year to solve existing problems and make the state function better. A bill is a proposed law. Bills may be introduced by lawmakers in either the house or the senate. In a recent session, bills introduced covered such topics as water rights, training required for child care workers, and farmers' markets.

When a bill is introduced, it is given a number and read twice in the house where it was proposed. It is then assigned to one or more committees for consideration. Each committee considers bills that are related to a certain subject. For example, in the House of Representatives, there is an Agriculture and Water Resources Committee.

Once in committee, a bill is discussed. At this point, public testimony is often invited, and people, companies, and organizations can give the committee their views about the

The Highest Capital City

Santa Fe is the highest capital city in the United States at 7,000 feet [2,134 m] above sea level.

bill. Committee members may make changes (amendments) to the bill. Then, they can recommend that the bill be passed, recommend that it not be passed, or send it back to the house where it originated without any recommendation.

If a committee recommends that a bill be passed, it is read a third time and then the entire house debates the bill. Amendments may be added at this time. Then, the members vote on the bill. In order for a bill to pass, it must receive a majority vote of the members present.

A bill that passes one house goes to the other house, where the same process is repeated. The second house considering the bill may make further changes to it. If the second house passes a changed version of the bill, then the bill goes to a conference committee. This committee, made up of members from both chambers, tries to resolve the differences between the two versions and work out a compromise. If they succeed, then a final version of the bill is sent back to both houses for their approval.

Once the two chambers have passed the same version of the bill, this final bill is sent to the governor. He or she can sign the bill, in which case it becomes law. If the governor disagrees with the bill, he or she can reject, or veto, it. A vetoed bill does not become law unless both chambers of the legislature again vote in favor of it, this time by a two-thirds majority. Such an action by the legislature is called overriding the governor's veto. A governor may also take no action on a bill. In that case, the bill becomes law three days after the governor receives it, provided that the legislature is still in session. When a bill is sent to the governor less than three days before the legislature adjourns, if the governor takes no action, the bill does not become law.

United States Senate and Congress

Like all other states, New Mexico voters choose people to represent them in the US Congress in Washington, DC. New Mexico voters elect two US Senators and three representatives in the US House of Representatives. Every state elects two senators, but the number of representatives is determined by each state's population.

New Mexico has more voters belonging to the Democratic Party than to the Republican Party. Almost 20 percent of New Mexicans are independent voters, who have not declared membership in either major political party. National, state, and county officials tend to be a mix of both Democrats and Republicans.

New Mexico is called a "bellwether" or "swing" state in presidential elections, meaning that New Mexican voters vote for different parties in national elections and almost always choose the winning candidate.

POLITICAL★FIGURES
FROM NEW MEXICO

Susana Martinez:
Governor of New Mexico, 2011–

In 2011, Susana Martinez became New Mexico's first female governor and the first Hispanic female elected governor in US history. She was reelected in November 2014. A former District Attorney, she was named by *Time* magazine as one of the 100 Most Influential People in the world in 2013.

William "Bill" Richardson III:
Governor, 2003–2011

William Blaine "Bill" Richardson III's impressive career included serving as a New Mexico Congressman (1982–1997), US Ambassador to the United Nations (1997–1998), Secretary of Energy (1998–2001), and as a two-term governor of New Mexico (2003–2011). He became one of the most prominent Hispanic politicians in the US (his mother is Mexican).

Tom Udall:
US Senator, 2009–

Tom Udall began serving as United States Senator in 2009, after two decades of public service as a US Representative and New Mexico's State Attorney General. He was reelected to a second term in 2014. He graduated from the University of New Mexico Law School in 1977.

MR. UDALL

NEW MEXICO
YOU CAN MAKE A DIFFERENCE

Contacting Lawmakers

All citizens can contact their government representatives to express their views. To e-mail the governor, go to: **www.governor.state.nm.us** and click on Contact the Governor under Quick Links.

To find your US senator, go to **www.senate.gov/general/contact_information/senators_cfm.cfm** or **www.house.gov/representatives** and click on the state list. Under New Mexico you will see both Senators listed, along with links to their websites.

To find your House of Representatives member, go to **www.house.gov/representatives** and click on N. Scroll to New Mexico. There is a link to each representative's website.

For state legislators, go to **www.nmlegis.gov/lcs/default.aspx**

Helping Teen Parents Stay In School

New Mexico has one of the highest rates of teen pregnancy in the country. Many teens who become pregnant and have babies leave high school and never receive their diplomas. That hurts a young mother's chance to provide a better life for her child.

In 2011, an Albuquerque-based group called Young Women United teamed with the ACLU (American Civil Liberties Union) of New Mexico to help these teen women stay in school. Many high schools marked students with unexcused absences when they missed school for doctor visits or to give birth. Students with too many unexcused absences were expelled from school. Even good students fell behind because teachers weren't letting them make up assignments.

The groups worked with the State Legislature to write a bill to create a new excused absence policy. The bill passed by a wide margin and became law in 2013. Now students receive additional days off to give birth and tend to their children's needs, helping them stay in school. State Senator Craig Brandt said that, while not supporting teen pregnancy, "We need to do everything we can to support young women who decide to keep their children."

A scientist at Los Alamos checks on honeybees being trained to detect bombs for the war on terror.

Making a Living

5

New Mexico's ancient peoples built extraordinary cities, sometimes hauling blocks of stone on their backs for long distances over rugged roads. Later, their descendants constructed elaborate irrigation systems to water their fields. Today, New Mexicans still have close ties to the land and its many gifts.

New Mexico's economy was once based on farming and ranching. Since the 1940s, that has changed, with manufacturing becoming more and more important. Manufacturing in New Mexico is different than in other states, however. There is no long history of factory buildings, smokestacks, or assembly lines. Instead, manufacturing is about mixing new technologies and ancient arts.

Living on the Land

From the earliest Mogollons, farming has been a New Mexican way of life. Crops grown today include hay, corn, wheat, cotton, pecans, and chiles. In the dry northeast, farmers rely on deep wells for water. In other dry areas, people raise cattle on long-established ranches. In the rugged northwest corner of the state, Navajos herd sheep.

The shortage of water and the presence of wild animals in many areas can make it hard to live off the land, however. For years, ranchers have argued with other concerned citizens about land and water use, as well as what to do about predators that kill their

Chili peppers are an important crop in New Mexico.

cattle and sheep. Cattle are allowed to graze on public land, but many people are opposed to this practice. They think the cattle use too much water and destroy the grasses and soil. Ranchers also say that they have a right to protect their herds from attacks by wild animals such as wolves, coyotes, and bears. So, in cattle country, ranchers have killed off many of these animals, a practice opposed by many environmentalists.

Natural Resources and Mining

In 1539, friar Marcos de Niza reported that New Mexico was "a land rich in gold, silver, and other wealth." Many Spaniards believed his words and came to the area hoping to find riches.

Mining on a significant scale did not begin until the early 1800s, however, when the Spanish started to take copper from the hills in Apache territory in the southwestern part of present-day New Mexico. They later mined gold and silver, but to this day, copper remains the state's top metal. It is used in plumbing pipes, electrical wires, and automobile parts.

Coal has been mined in New Mexico since the 1800s. Other minerals mined include **potash**, used to make fertilizer, and manganese, a metal used in making steel. New Mexico has deposits of uranium, which is a mineral that fuels nuclear power plants, nuclear submarines, and other warships. Petroleum and natural gas are also found in the state. These fuels help supply the nation's energy needs.

Mining can be hard on the environment. Mining companies have agreed to clean up their waste, but it is not always easy. One former miner has noted, "Mining here has not had so glorified a history … There's no way around it, some of the things the environmentalists say are true—mining is very unsightly. Devastating. But it is controlled, and it has to be."

Technology Grows

Technology came to New Mexico in part because of its remote and open spaces. During World War II, the United States needed to build up its military capability. At Los Alamos, hidden in the remote Jemez Mountains, the government set up a top-secret laboratory to develop nuclear weapons. About 300 miles (500 km) away, the first atomic bomb was tested in 1945. The test site is part of what is now called the White Sands Missile Range, which the US military still uses to test rockets and other advanced weapons being developed.

Today, many technology products are not made in secret. The government laboratories led to the development of a "talent pool" of scientists, engineers, and other technologically skilled workers in New Mexico. After World War II, a number of them stayed and worked on other products, such as computers, robots, and energy production.

Kirtland Air Force Base is one of the many military bases in New Mexico. Air Force CV-22 Ospreys take off at the facility near Albuquerque.

★ 10 KEY INDUSTRIES ★

Aerospace

1. Aerospace

The aerospace industry continues to grow in New Mexico thanks to an ideal climate, clear flying conditions, restricted air space, and advanced testing facilities. Spaceport America is owned by the State of New Mexico and is the world's first commercial spaceport.

2. Chilis

Chilis have been grown in New Mexico for at least four centuries. In recent decades, New Mexico has produced more chilis than any other state. After a harvest, people hang strands of red chilis, called *ristras*, outside to dry.

3. Copper

In 1800, an Apache warrior gave a Spanish soldier an arrow point made of copper. Significant amounts of copper have been mined in New Mexico ever since. Now most of the copper is used in making electrical wires and plumbing pipes.

Dairy Products

4. Dairy Products

New Mexico's climate helps make it one of the nation's top ten dairy-producing states. A Roswell cheese factory is the largest maker of mozzarella cheese in the country. It uses four million gallons (fifteen million liters) of milk a day.

5. Electricity

New Mexico produces more electricity than it uses. Electricity produced from coal and other sources in New Mexico is distributed to consumers in Texas, Arizona, California, and Utah. In 2013, New Mexico ranked fifth in the nation in utility-scale electricity generation from solar energy.

NEW MEXICO ★ ★ ★

6. Health Care

New Mexicans over age sixty-five are the fastest-growing segment of the state's population, leading to more need for good health care. The health services industry now employs the largest percentage of New Mexico's workforce and is growing steadily.

7. Military

Military spending contributes a great deal to the New Mexico economy. The state hosts four major military bases, including three air force bases (Cannon, Holloman, and Kirtland) as well as an Army testing range (White Sands Missile Range).

8. Oil and Natural Gas

New Mexico is the sixth-ranked state in crude oil production, seventh in natural gas, twelfth in coal, and eleventh in total energy production. More of the state's income from mining comes from oil and natural gas than from any other source.

9. Science Laboratories

Many high-technology laboratories conduct scientific research, working in areas such as energy, pharmaceutical products, nuclear weapons, human genetics, computers, and robotics. Los Alamos National Laboratory is one of the largest science and technology labs in the world.

10. Tourism

Tourists flock to New Mexico to enjoy its scenic beauty, outdoor sports, arts and crafts, and cultural celebrations. Tourism ranks as one of New Mexico's largest industries.

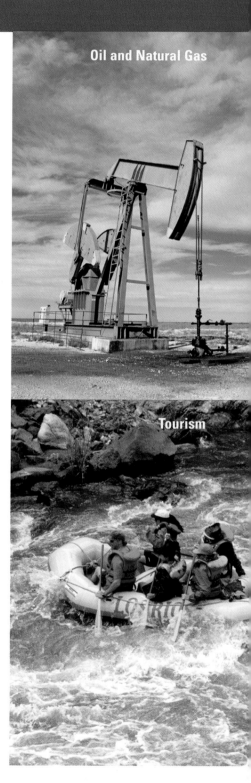

Oil and Natural Gas

Tourism

Recipe for Mexican Hot Chocolate

Chocolate was introduced to Spanish settlers by the native peoples of what is now the southwestern United States, Mexico and Central America. The Native Americans also used the roasted beans to make a chocolate drink.

Some people think that this Mexican hot chocolate tastes much better than the traditional American version. First, you make it from real chocolate. Then, you spice it up with cinnamon, vanilla, and sometimes a kick of chile. Here's a recipe for four people.

What You Need

5 cups (1,183 milliliters) whole milk

1 tablespoon (14.8 mL) or more ancho chile (or red chile) powder (don't use a powder that contains anything except ground chile peppers)

1 vanilla bean, split lengthwise

3-inch (7.62 cm) piece cinnamon

8 ounces (237 mL) unsweetened or bittersweet chocolate, chopped

Honey and/or brown sugar

What to Do

- In a medium saucepan over medium heat, combine the milk, chile powder, vanilla bean, and cinnamon. Cook just until it comes to a boil, and then reduce the heat to low.

- Add the chocolate and whisk until it dissolves.

- Remove the vanilla bean and cinnamon, and then pour the chocolate into mugs. Serve the chocolate with honey and brown sugar on the side, allowing your guests to sweeten it themselves.

Antennas at the Very Large Array pick up radio waves given off by objects in space.

Scientists at Los Alamos National Laboratory now work on a wide range of projects, including research related to nuclear weapons, advanced computers, and renewable energy sources. Another laboratory, Sandia National Laboratories in Albuquerque, was started in 1949 as an extension of the work being done in Los Alamos. Today, scientists at Sandia focus on issues of US defense and homeland security. But they also do research on climate change and on alternatives to fossil fuels.

Government facilities also contract out some of their activities to private companies. As a result, in recent decades dozens of private companies in the aerospace industry have located in New Mexico, employing thousands of workers to build equipment and conduct research. The skilled work force has also helped other industries start up in cities such as Albuquerque, Roswell, and Las Cruces. There, scientists and other workers make computer parts, medical devices, and pharmaceutical products.

Home on the Range

Even though New Mexico's economy is no longer based on ranching and farming, there are still far more cows and sheep in the state than there are people.

An example of a large project is the Very Large Array (VLA). On a vast plain about 50 miles (80 km) from the town of Socorro, The National Science Foundation constructed twenty-seven dish antennas, each more than 80 feet (25 m) in diameter, to form a huge Y shape. From a distance, writer Henry Shukman claimed, they seemed to be a "fleet of white

Native crafts such as woven baskets are important to the state economy.

sailing boats." In a way they are. But these giant dishes sail the universe instead of the sea. Using radio waves instead of light waves, the dishes give scientists regular information about stars and galaxies thousands of light-years from Earth. A light-year is the distance that something moving at the speed of light would cover in one year.

Another important, though very different, form of manufacturing comes from the native people of the state. Native American arts and crafts have long been an important part of New Mexico's economy. In ancient times, Native American baskets, pottery, jewelry, blankets, and other items made from woven fabrics were valuable trade goods. The same remains true today.

Tourism

The connection between New Mexico, its land, and its history can be seen in the success of its tourism industry, one of the state's largest sources of income. Many people come to visit New Mexico to see the rugged mountain ranges, deserts, canyons, and scenic rivers. They enjoy skiing, river rafting, fishing, hunting, and mountain biking. Skiers flock to Taos, Angel Fire, and the Mescalero Apache resort. In the Gila Wilderness, mountain bikers compete in international races.

Visitors are also drawn to the state's cultural variety. On summer nights, the Santa Fe Opera House is filled with music lovers. The New Mexico Museum of Art in Santa Fe is the oldest museum in the state. It houses more than twenty thousand works of art by Southwest artists. The Museum of International Folk Art, also in Santa Fe, is home to the world's largest collection of folk art from around the world.

Tourists also enjoy Native American ceremonies and Spanish fiestas across the state. Thousands of tourists visit the multi-storied adobe buildings of the Taos Pueblo every year.

The Santa Fe Indian Market, held on a weekend in August each year, hosts around one hundred thousand visitors. Chef Mark Miller has said, "Indian Market is awash with color, sound, energy, and fragrances."

Some of New Mexico's residents are unsure whether the tourist industry is truly good for the state. Some believe that too many visitors decide to stay. A resident of the village of Angel Fire has commented, "Everyone who moves here wishes they were the last … People here … are afraid it will get crowded and be nothing but traffic jams!" These people believe that too many newcomers will harm the balance of nature. Yet others believe that income from tourism keeps a special way of life alive. Former Albuquerque mayor Martin Chavez has said, "It is economic vitality which gives us the means to preserve our natural and cultural riches, the habits of the heart."

Protecting the land remains part of New Mexico's heritage. One famous symbol of safeguarding wilderness areas is the cartoon character Smokey Bear. The Smokey character was based on a bear cub found in New Mexico in 1950. It had been injured in a forest fire caused by careless people. The cub was rescued and lived a long life. Ever since then, in advertisements and posters, Smokey Bear has been reminding people, "Only you can prevent forest fires."

New Mexico has changed quite a bit since the first Spanish explorers encountered the Pueblos. However, New Mexicans continue to prove that they can find solutions that preserve their values, culture, and traditions. As the New Mexico state motto proclaims, "It grows as it goes."

The Santa Fe Opera House was completed in 1998.

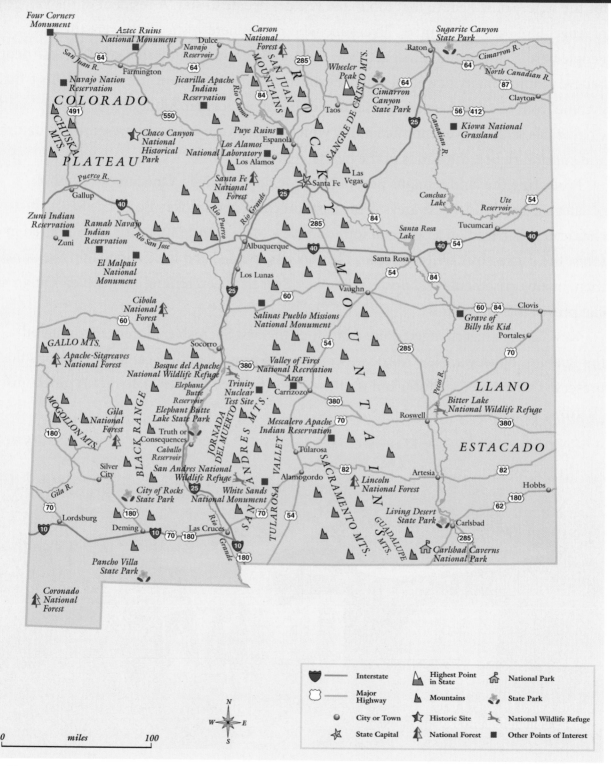

Four Corners Monument

Aztec Ruins National Monument

Dulce

Navajo Reservoir

Carson National Forest

Sugarite Canyon State Park

Raton

Cimarron R.

North Canadian R.

San Juan R.

64

64

Farmington

Jicarilla Apache Indian Reservation

Rio Chama

SAN JUAN MOUNTAINS

285

Wheeler Peak

64

Cimarron Canyon State Park

25

87

Clayton

Navajo Nation Reservation

COLORADO

491

CHUSKA MTS.

550

Chaco Canyon National Historical Park

84

PLATEAU

Puerco R.

Puye Ruins

Los Alamos National Laboratory

Espanola

Los Alamos

Taos

ROCKY

SANGRE DE CRISTO MTS.

56 412

Kiowa National Grassland

Canadian R.

Las Vegas

Gallup

40

Santa Fe National Forest

Rio Grande

Rio Puerco

Santa Fe

25

Conchas Lake

Ute Reservoir

54

Zuni Indian Reservation

Ramah Navajo Indian Reservation

Rio San Jose

285

84

Santa Rosa Lake

Tucumcari

Zuni

El Malpais National Monument

Albuquerque

40

Santa Rosa

40 54

40

Cibola National Forest

Los Lunas

25

60

Vaughn

54

84

60 84

Clovis

GALLO MTS.

60

Salinas Pueblo Missions National Monument

M

Grave of Billy the Kid

Portales

Apache-Sitgreaves National Forest

Socorro

O

54

285

70

LLANO

Bosque del Apache National Wildlife Refuge

380

Valley of Fires National Recreation Area

U

Bitter Lake National Wildlife Refuge

MOGOLLON MTS.

Elephant Butte Reservoir

Trinity Nuclear Test Site

Carrizozo

380

N

Roswell

ESTACADO

180

Gila National Forest

Elephant Butte Lake State Park

Mescalero Apache Indian Reservation

70

T

380

Truth or Consequences

BLACK RANGE

JORNADA DEL MUERTO

Caballo Reservoir

Tularosa

A

Artesia

82

Silver City

San Andres National Wildlife Refuge

SAN ANDRES MTS.

Alamogordo

82

Hobbs

Gila R.

25

City of Rocks State Park

White Sands National Monument

Lincoln National Forest

I

62 180

70

180

TULAROSA VALLEY

54

SACRAMENTO MTS.

N

Living Desert State Park

Carlsbad

Lordsburg

Deming

10 70

Las Cruces

Rio Grande

10

GUADALUPE MTS.

285

10

180

Carlsbad Caverns National Park

Pancho Villa State Park

Coronado National Forest

NEW MEXICO ★ ★ ★
MAP SKILLS

1. Locate New Mexico's state capital on the map. What is the closest town or city to the east?

2. What two interstate highways meet near Albuquerque?

3. What is the name of the large river that runs north/south all the way through New Mexico?

4. What National Wildlife Refuge lies south of Billy the Kid's Grave?

5. Carlsbad Caverns National Park is closest to what New Mexico border: North, East, South, or West?

6. What National Forest is closest to Los Alamos National Laboratory?

7. Gila National Forest is located close to what mountain range?

8. Kiowa National Grassland can be found in which corner of the state: northeast, northwest, southeast or southwest?

9. What is the highest point in New Mexico?

10. What Native American Reservation is closest to El Malpais National Monument?

Bitter Lake Wildlife Refuge

Wheeler Peak

10. Ramah Navajo Indian Reservation
9. Wheeler Peak, at 13,167 feet (4,013 meters)
8. Northeast
7. Mogollon Mountains
6. Santa Fe National Forest
5. South
4. Bitter Lake National Wildlife Refuge
3. The Rio Grande
2. Interstates 25 and 40
1. Las Vegas (New Mexico, not Nevada!)

State Flag, Seal, and Song

New Mexico's state flag is yellow with the state emblem, the Zia, in red. The emblem is styled after the Zia Pueblo's symbol for the sun. The sun's rays represent central elements of the natural and spiritual worlds. Four groups of four lines stand for the four directions, the four parts of the day, the four stages of life, and the four seasons. The circle at the center symbolizes life.

The state seal was adopted in 1912. The two eagles in the center—the large American bald eagle and the smaller Mexican eagle—stand for the transfer of New Mexico from Mexico to the United States. The American eagle holds arrows in its talons, while the Mexican eagle has a snake in its beak, a reference to an ancient Aztec myth. A scroll beneath both eagles contains the state motto, written in Latin. "*Crescit Eundo*" translates as "It grows as it goes."

"O Fair New Mexico," the state song of New Mexico, was officially selected in 1917. The author, Elizabeth Garrett, was the daughter of former Lincoln County Sheriff Pat Garrett, the man who killed Billy the Kid. Lyrics can be found at: **nmstatehood.unm.edu/node/78792**

Glossary

adobe Sun-dried brick made of clay and straw.

arroyos Dry creekbeds or riverbeds that can flood during rainstorms or with melting snow.

hogans The traditional dwellings and ceremonial structures of the Navajos of Arizona and New Mexico. Early hogans were dome-shaped buildings with log, or occasionally stone, frameworks.

kiva A Pueblo Native American ceremonial structure that is usually round and partly underground.

mesa A flat-topped hill with steep sides.

nomadic People who roam frequently from place to place.

omnivorous Animals that feed on both plants and animals.

potash A compound containing potassium obtained from wood ash that is used in fertilizers and for other purposes.

pueblo Flat-roofed stone or adobe houses in groups sometimes several stories high. Also used to refer to a village of pueblo buildings and the Native peoples who built and lived in them.

sovereignty A country's independent authority and the right to govern itself.

tuff Rock that is formed from volcanic ash.

UFO An unidentified flying object, sometimes thought to be an alien craft from outer space.

UNESCO The United Nations Educational, Scientific, and Cultural Organization, an agency that sponsors programs to promote education, communication, and the arts.

World Heritage Site A natural or man-made site, area, or structure which has great international importance and deserves special protection. Sites are chosen by UNESCO's World Heritage Convention.

More About New Mexico

BOOKS

Keegan, Marcia. *Taos Pueblo and Its Sacred Blue Lake*. Santa Fe, NM: Clear Light Publishers, 2010.

Lasky, Kathryn. *Georgia Rises: A Day in the Life of Georgia O'Keeffe*. New York: Farrar, Straus and Giroux, 2009.

Lourie, Peter. *The Lost World of the Anasazi: Exploring the Mysteries of Chaco Canyon*. Honesdale, PA: Boyds Mills Press, 2007.

Lyon, Robin. *The Spanish Missions of New Mexico*. New York: Children's Press, 2010.

WEBSITES

Indian Pueblo Cultural Center:
www.indianpueblo.org

New Mexico State Government Official Website:
www.newmexico.gov

New Mexico Tourism Department Website for Families:
www.newmexico.org/true-family-fun

ABOUT THE AUTHORS

Ruth Bjorklund lives on Bainbridge Island, a ferry ride away from Seattle, Washington, and two ferry rides away from Skagway, Alaska.

Ellen H. Todras is a freelance writer and editor. She loves history and enjoys bringing it to life for young people. She lives with her husband in Eugene, Oregon.

Gerard (Gerry) Boehme was born in New York City, graduated from The Newhouse School at Syracuse University, and lives on Long Island with his wife and two children.

Index

Page numbers in **boldface** are illustrations. Entries in **boldface** are glossary terms.

Index